I CAN'T!

LEARNING ABOUT TRYING NEW THINGS

Katherine Eason

FOX EYE
PUBLISHING

Alice was afraid to try **NEW THINGS**. She **WORRIED** that she might make a **MISTAKE**. She didn't know that mistakes help us to learn. She didn't know that being good at things takes practice.

Alice was **TOO AFRAID** to give new things a go.

Alice and her mum took Oscar to his gymnastics class. He did handstands and cartwheels. **IT LOOKED FUN!**

Alice **WISHED** that she could do gymnastics. But she was **TOO AFRAID** to give it a go.

Mum and Alice baked some cakes. The cakes looked funny and wonky. They laughed. Alice decorated the cakes. They tasted delicious.

Mum gave Alice a sticker for making an **EFFORT**.

Mum and Alice made some glove puppets. Alice's puppet had wonky arms and a funny face. Mum said it was her favourite one.

Next, they had a jelly and spoon race. Alice ran fast. She dropped her jelly. She put it back on the spoon and walked to the finish.

Mum gave Alice a sticker for **NOT GIVING UP** and for learning from her mistakes.

Mum and Alice made a book and some stickers about the NEW THINGS Alice had tried. They talked about when Alice learnt to ride her bike.

At first, she had training wheels. But with practice, she didn't need them.

Mum said it was OK to make mistakes. That's how we learn to do things well. The important thing is **HAVING A GO**. Mum said Alice was good at trying new things now.

Alice went to the gymnastics open day. They did forward rolls. Alice's roll went sideways. But that was OK. Alice was learning, and she was having fun.

Alice **FELT GOOD**. She had learnt to **GIVE** new things a **GO**.

Words and Behaviour

Alice was too afraid to try new things in this story and that caused a lot of problems.

EFFORT

TRY

NEW THINGS

WORRIED

There are a lot of words to do with trying new things in this book. Can you remember all of them?

MISTAKE

AFRAID

Let's talk about feelings and manners

This series helps children to understand difficult emotions and behaviours and how to manage them. The characters in the series have been created to show emotions and behaviours that are often seen in young children, and which can be difficult to manage.

I Can't!

The story in this book examines the reasons for trying new things. It looks at why trying new things is important and how trying new things helps people to learn new skills and have fun.

How to use this book

You can read this book with one child or a group of children. The book can be used to begin a discussion around complex behaviour such as trying new things.

The book is also a reading aid, with enlarged and repeated words to help children to develop their reading skills.

How to read the story

Before beginning the story, ensure that the children you are reading to are relaxed and focused.

Take time to look at the enlarged words and the illustrations, and discuss what this book might be about before reading the story.

New words can be tricky for young children to approach. Sounding them out first, slowly and repeatedly, can help children to learn the words and become familiar with them.

How to discuss the story

When you have finished reading the story, use these questions and discussion points to examine the theme of the story with children and explore the emotions and behaviour within it:
- What do you think the story was about?
- Have you been in a situation in which you were afraid to try something new? What was that situation?
- Do you think trying new things doesn't matter? Why?
- Do you think trying new things is important? Why?
- What could go wrong if you don't try new things?

Titles in the series

 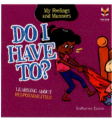  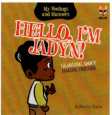 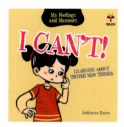
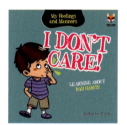    
 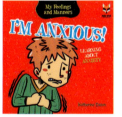  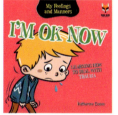 
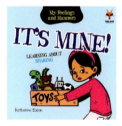   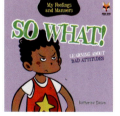 

First published in 2023 by Fox Eye Publishing
Unit 31, Vulcan House Business Centre,
Vulcan Road, Leicester, LE5 3EF
www.foxeyepublishing.com

Copyright © 2023 Fox Eye Publishing
All rights reserved. No portion of this book may be reproduced in any form without permission from the publisher, except as permitted by U.K. copyright law.

Author: Katherine Eason
Art director: Paul Phillips
Cover designer: Emily Bailey
Editor: Jenny Rush

All illustrations by Novel

ISBN 978-1-80445-173-1

Printed in China